Rookie
Read-About® Geography

Living in the Forest

By Donna Loughran

Consultant
Nanci R. Vargus, Ed.D.
Assistant Professor of Literacy
University of Indianapolis, Indianapolis, Indiana

Children's Press®
A Division of Scholastic Inc.
New York   Toronto   London   Auckland   Sydney
Mexico City   New Delhi   Hong Kong
Danbury, Connecticut

Designer: Herman Adler Design
Photo Researcher: Caroline Anderson
The photo on the cover shows the Yanomamo Indian village in the Amazon.

Library of Congress Cataloging-in-Publication Data

Loughran, Donna.
  Living in the forest / by Donna Loughran.
    p. cm. – (Rookie read-about geography)
Includes index.
Summary: Describes how people make their homes in or near the forests of
the world and how their lives are affected by the woods.
  ISBN 0-516-22740-8 (lib. bdg)   0-516-27330-2 (pbk.)
  1. Forests and forestry–Juvenile literature. 2. Forest
ecology–Juvenile literature. [1. Forests and forestry. 2. Forest
ecology. 3. Ecology.] I. Title. II. Series.
  SD376.L68 2003
  577.3–dc21
                              2003000455

CHILDREN'S PRESS, and ROOKIE READ-ABOUT®,
and associated logos are trademarks and or registered trademarks
of Scholastic Library Publishing. SCHOLASTIC and associated logos
are trademarks and or registered trademarks of Scholastic Inc.
1 2 3 4 5 6 7 8 9 10 R 12 11 10 09 08 07 06 05 04 03

Whoosh goes the wind in the forest.

Chirp. There's a bird in the tree. The forest is a place for trees and birds.

Rose-breasted grosbeak

It is a place for you, too.

There are cool forests and warm, wet forests. Each kind of forest has its own kinds of plants and animals.

Grey squirrel

Breathe deeply. Do you smell the pine trees that grow in this forest? Their leaves look like needles.

The cones on their
branches hold seeds.

Snowshoe hare

In the winter, this forest is cold.

People wear thick clothes to stay warm. Some forest animals have thick fur to stay warm.

In the Black Forest, fir
trees grow near the top of
mountains. These dark trees
give the forest its name.

13

In the autumn (AW-tuhm), oak, maple, and beech trees have bright colors.

Look up.

See the bright red, yellow, and orange leaves before they fall.

15

People live and work in the
Black Forest. They make toys
and other things from wood.

Wait for the cuckoo in
this clock to come out.

People also come to the
forest to play. In the summer,
they ride bikes and sail boats.

In the winter, they ski
down mountains and
across snowy fields.

ATLANTIC
OCEAN

Amazon River

Amazon Rain Forest

BRAZIL

SOUTH
AMERICA

PACIFIC
OCEAN

North

West ✦ East

South

SCALE 1 inch = 700 miles

0   Miles   700

0   Kilometers   1100

Snow does not fall in all forests. In Brazil, there is a large rain forest. This forest is warm and wet all year.

It is the largest forest in the world. Many kinds of trees grow here.

The Amazon River flows through the forest. It is a very long river.

Toucan

Many kinds of animals
also live in the rain forest.

Bats and snakes live there.
Birds and anteaters do, too.

Anteater

People have lived in the rain forest for a long time. Today, some people live like people did long ago.

They hunt and fish. They use plants for medicine and food.

Rain forest people care for their land and the things that live there. The forest is their home.

What is your home like?

Words You Know

Amazon River

autumn

cones

cuckoo

needles   rain forest

ski

Index

About the Author

Donna Loughran is an artist, writer, and multimedia designer. She lives in Austin, Texas.

Photo Credits

Photographs © 2003: Corbis Images: 25 (Tom Brakefield), 18 (Tom Nebbia); Dembinsky Photo Assoc.: 9, 30 bottom left (Michael P. Gadomski), 4 (Randall B. Henne), 24 (Doug Locke); Peter Arnold Inc.: 23, 30 top left (Jacques Janquox), 19, 31 bottom (Helga Lade), cover, 28 (Luiz C. Marigo), 16 (Werner H. Muller), 27 (Bios/M. Roggo); Photo Researchers, NY: 21, 31 top right (Gregory G. Dimijian), 10 (Tom & Pat Leeson); The Image Works: 8, 31 top left (Elizabeth Crews), 29 (Michael J. Doolittle), 15, 30 top right (Eastcott-Momatiuk), 3 (Esbin-Anderson), 12 (Margot Granitsas), 5 (Ray Stott), 17, 30 bottom right (Topham); Visuals Unlimited/Gary Carter: 7.

Maps by Bob Italiano